EDITORIAL EXPECTATIONS
Yours and Theirs

JUDITH REVEAL

*"You write to communicate to the hearts and minds
of others what's burning inside you,
and we edit to let the fire show through the smoke."*
—Arthur Plotnik

THE-EFA.ORG

Copyright © 2018 by Judith Reveal and the Editorial Freelancers Association
New York, NY, USA.

The EFA is a national nonprofit volunteer association of professionals who provide freelance editorial services to the publishing and communications industries. EFA members live in the United States and abroad and are experienced in a wide range of professional skills, subject areas, and media.

Members include abstractors, copyeditors, designers, desktop publishing experts, editors, indexers, manuscript evaluators, picture researchers, project managers, textbook development editors, translators, and writers.

While every precaution has been taken in the preparation of this book, the publisher and the author assume no responsibility for errors or omissions or for damages resulting from the use of the information contained herein.

All rights reserved. No part of this book may be reproduced in any form or by any means without the prior written consent of the publisher, except for brief quotes used in reviews.

ISBN: 978-1-880407-01-1
Ebook ISBN: 978-1-880407-07-3

Your purchase of this book benefits the Editorial Freelancers Association, a nonprofit organization.

Judith Reveal
justcreativewriting.com
nyjournalofbooks.com/judith.reveal
amazon.com/author/judithreveal
facebook.com/judy.reveal

Contents

Acknowledgements	v
Dedication	vii
Introduction	ix
Expectations	1
Editor	1
Author	2
Process	3
Changes	4
Money	6
Contracts	7
Deadlines	8
Communication	10
References	10
In Conclusion . . .	13
Bibliography	15
About the Author	16

Acknowledgements

I would like to take this opportunity to recognize Roy Bartels for his keen eye for things that have gone amiss. Had he not looked at this manuscript, I would have overlooked several grammatically incorrect items, punctuation errors, and organizational questions.

My thanks also to Kim Carlson, Lisa Falkner, and Martha Hofstetter for looking for problems in this work! Without the extra sets of eyes, this work would have failed.

I would also like to thank the Editorial Freelancers Association for the opportunity to share my thoughts on expectations for editors and authors. This booklet and the many other informational booklets published by the EFA provide a world of information for editors, authors, and all the wordsmiths of the world.

*Over the past ten years it has been my honor to work with
many authors (some new, some more experienced),
and I have had the pleasure of teaching them,
and more importantly, learning from them.
I dedicate this work to these friends and collaborators
and thank them for their patience with me.*

Introduction

Words. I love words. They are informative, curious, humorous, mysterious, tragic, academic—it doesn't matter whether they are used in fiction or nonfiction, essays or poetry—words play an important role in our lives.

As a reader and reviewer of books for the New York Journal of Books (nyjournalofbooks.com), I often see words that drive me to read on; words that fit together like a lovely jigsaw puzzle to create an interesting story, or a strong protagonist, or words that explain a curious concept, like "quarks."

But I sometimes find myself reading words that stop me short. When I read, I expect to be entertained and engaged, and when that doesn't happen, I question if the author and editor expressed and met one another's expectations. Expectations are not predictions; they might not be asked and answered using that specific word; they might be implied rather than spoken. They require work on the part of both parties; both the editor and the author need to share their expectations as well as question those of the other before the project begins. Once expectations are identified and resolved, the difference between the shelf-sitter and the page-turner will begin to evolve.

Establishing a successful relationship between the author and the editor depends on transparency between both parties. And what does "transparency" mean? Both parties should ask the questions that will affect their relationship, and the answers should be clear and concise. As Jon Harrison points out, "Of course, we should be clear right from the outset that author and editor are on the same side; they are, or should be, a team working toward a common goal."[1]

As both an author and an editor, I have experienced both sides of the relationship when the expectations to produce a top-notch book are raised, discussed, agreed upon, and resolved. It's that communication that ultimately makes the book interesting.

An author should have some idea of what questions to ask when he approaches an editor. He should not accept an editor at face value but should ask pertinent questions about how his work will be handled and what he will get back at the end of the process. Erin Wilcox clarifies several author expectations: "As a client, you can help the good-faith negotiation get off on the right foot by attending to the following:

- Define your goals for the project
- Take stock of where you are in the creative/publishing process
- Research the market for independent editorial services
- Determine a rough budget for your project"[2]

The editor, on the other hand, should be professional and transparent about her work: what she does, how she does it, and what she will return to the author at the end of the process.

Knowing how to approach an editor, and encourage an author, should be an enjoyable dance toward establishing a relationship and a successful project for both parties.

The search for an editor can be helped along through the use of editing groups such as the Editorial Freelancers Association, Scribendi, or Upwork—organizations that gather a multitude of editors under one umbrella, allowing the author the opportunity to gather relevant information with just a few keystrokes.

I would be remiss if I did not comment on a variety of editing options available to the author, including editing software such as Hemingway Editor, Grammarly, Autocrit, etc. The level of human interaction with editing software, however, is non-existent. This is not to say that editing software does not offer an initial step up to actions such as proofreading

---

1 *Author and Editor Together: Building the Best Manuscript*, 4
2 *Building Successful Freelancer-Client Relationships*, 9

Editorial Expectations

and grammar checking, but it cannot replace the initial and ongoing relationship between editor and author.

My goal for this booklet is to share my insight from both positions, and give both the author and the editor a picture from the other side. To this end, I discuss a series of topics that are important, as they address expectations for both participants. There is no particular order for discussing these expectations, since each holds its own level of importance.

So, let us begin this journey . . .

Expectations

Before getting into the details, a few words about why *expectations* are important!

Editor

Within moments of connecting with a potential client, an experienced editor will know what direction the conversation, and the request for assistance, will take. Previous clients and a variety of projects will have prepared the editor for each new job that comes along. Her expectations will not have changed, but she will be prepared for the questions that need to be asked.

So, what is an editor? In brief, it's someone who works with an author or publisher to improve a piece of writing. However, the role of the editor is quite broad and encompasses many services. A developmental editor may work with an author before a single word is written to help develop their ideas, while a copyeditor takes a written work and improves the grammar, consistency, and perhaps even the readability of the work. The editor may also have experience such as being a published author, book reviewer, or a book indexer, practices that add to her knowledge base. The bottom line? The editor is there on behalf of both the author and audience to make sure that a piece of writing communicates as effectively as possible.

As Betsy Lerner says, "Every prose writer has his own rhythms, from sentence structure to the length of paragraphs and chapter, and the editor must help him use that form to its most powerful effect . . . The art of editing is a dance one engages in with the author to help him achieve the best results."[3]

The editor's responsibility is to ensure that the story remains true to the author's voice. This may include telephone conversations, Skype, or perhaps a face-to-face over coffee to make sure those suggestions are clear and concise.

What does the editor not do? And this is a very important question that the author must know the answer to—the editor is not an agent, a publisher, or a publicist, unless she states otherwise at the beginning of the relationship. The editor will not be responsible for marketing the work, unless that is also agreed upon up front and is included in the contract. The editor has one goal—to work with the author to ensure that the end result is the best possible work for the readers' enjoyment.

The editor's responsibilities are the foundation for the author/editor relationship, primarily because the editor is experienced not only in working with words, but also anticipating the author's needs.

Author

Betsy Lerner brings home the discussion of what authors expect with: "All writers have a fantasy of who their editor will be and what the relationship will be like. In the best cases, the pairing is as mutually agreeable as a good friendship, in which each party feels ennobled by the other's company."[4]

The new author's expectations are usually simple. "Can you edit my manuscript and what will you charge?" A newer writer may be dipping his feet into the deep end of the pool without knowing what questions to ask, other than the basics. This writer will rely on the editor to guide him through the complexities of editing; he will expect trust and respect from the editor. Through this guidance more of the author's questions will begin to rise to the surface, raising expectations he may not have realized.

The experienced author's expectations will be a bit more detailed. "How will you edit my manuscript, how long will it take, what can I expect back from you, and what will it cost?" This writer may be a returning

---

3 *The Forest for the Trees*, 196-197
4 *The Forest for the Trees*, 209

client, in which case he will be familiar and comfortable with the process and the editor, and for the most part, the cost.

In either case, the author will still expect his work to be handled professionally and with care.

Process

The editing process may be a maze of sorts—it is a complex activity to accomplish (editor) and may be a complicated one to understand (author). The editor must comprehend the story set before her, while the author must untie the Gordian Knot returned to him.

Editor

The first step is to determine if the process will be a basic copyedit for grammar, spelling, consistency, and punctuation, or a deeper copyedit that will also include fact checking or rewording of awkward phrases, or still yet, a line edit that gets into creativity, style, and language. Without knowing the story, the editor must rely on a conversation with the author to determine which edit is most appropriate, and the project cannot move forward until both parties agree to the best approach.

Once this has been determined, the next question is: electronic or hard copy edit? In today's electronic supremacy in everything we do, most editors will work with electronic editing equipment such as the tracking function found in Word, or track in Pages on Mac.

Electronic editing has an abundance of pros: it saves time printing the manuscript and the cost of shipping; it allows the editor to embed suggestions, comments, deletions, and additions directly into the manuscript. This could be something as simple as adding or deleting punctuation, or as major as a lengthy comment questioning something in the manuscript. Electronic editing can be simple for the editor to do and for the author to understand.

But there are drawbacks to electronic editing as well. Studies have shown that electronic editing may make it easier to overlook errors because the material on the screen may be limited to one or two paragraphs or a set number of lines, and moving back and forth between screens can become tedious and awkward.

Editing hard copy, on the other hand, is easier for the editor to see one, two, or more pages at a time. The drawback to editing hard copy is the use of standard editing "code" used to indicate such things as "insert" "delete" "capital letter" "lower case," etc. These markings have been around for decades and most editors will be familiar with them—most authors will not.

The editor may have previous experience with either hard copy or electronic editing and may have a preference, but she should anticipate that the author may not be familiar with these options and should clarify the advantages and disadvantages of both. If the editor has a preference of editing style, she should explain the pros and cons of each style, and why she has that preference.

Author

The initial discussion of proofing, copyediting, or line editing may be daunting to a new author, and will raise a multitude of questions not previously anticipated. Once these options are explained, and the questions answered, the author may still have no idea which is better—hard copy editing or electronic editing. In order to make the appropriate decision, the author should make sure he understands the pros and cons of each.

Once the manuscript is returned with comments, either in hard copy or electronically, the author should anticipate that the revision will take time; revising a hard copy edit will require more attention and time to incorporate changes. The electronic edit allows the author to accept or reject the embedded suggestions with just the flick of the wrist, although this comes with an inherent risk. The responsibility falls to the author to read every page, every line, every word of the edited document to ensure that he agrees with everything the editor has proposed.

Changes

As authors we cannot edit our own work—we are too close to it; it is too easy to miss both the major and the minor points because we are so familiar with the twists and turns of the story. Editors will expect to make or suggest changes; authors should anticipate these suggestions and consider if the suggestions are right for the story.

Editorial Expectations

Editor

An experienced editor will know that the first draft will have an abundance of flaws and will expect problems to surface in the manuscript. She should be prepared to discuss these issues with the author.

What the author sees in his mind while writing the story is not necessarily what the editor sees in her mind while reading the story. To accomplish this mirror image, the editor will anticipate selecting the right word(s) to help the author convey his vision to the reader.

The editor owes it to the author and the reader to ensure that the picture put forward through editing is not only engaging but also clear. She understands that giving creative criticism is sometimes difficult, and she may walk a fine line to be supportive and honest with the author while also presenting an engaging story for the reader. It is not the editor's responsibility to rewrite an author's story, but to collaborate with that author.

If, as the editor is moving through the manuscript, she identifies problems with the story, if she feels it is disorganized, she has a responsibility to bring this to the author's attention. If, however, the author believes that accepting the suggested changes would drive the work in the wrong direction, he is not obligated to take the editor's suggestions. If the editor's interpretation of the author's work requires changes of any magnitude, it may then be beneficial to ask for a meeting—either face-to-face or via telephone or Skype or any other means available—and the editor should detail what she sees and how and why she feels it should be changed. The editor makes the suggestions based on her experience; the author must determine if those suggestions work for his story. Again, the editor's job is not to rewrite the story, but to help enhance it. It is important for both the editor and the author to keep in mind that changes are only suggestions and both the editor and the author need to receive suggestions without taking comments personally.

With regard to questions the editor might ask in the manuscript, in my experience when I ask a question, I generally do not require an answer. My goal is to make the author think about *why* I asked it in the first place. Did I see something in the writing that was out of place? Does something not make sense? I edit electronically and when something comes to my attention that either I do not understand, or I think the author should address, I will comment in as much detail as I can, in a tracking balloon, but I expect the author to think about that question or comment. I discourage the author from arbitrarily taking my questions or comments as gospel.

Author
If the author does not understand a particular question or comment, he should give serious thought to those comments because only he knows the story from beginning to end. He should question the suggestion, not assume the editor is right. The author should never be afraid to question why an editor is suggesting a particular change. More importantly, the author should not be afraid to reject any suggestion that just doesn't work or he does not understand, even after a conversation.

Money

Let's get right down to the nitty-gritty of the editing discussion — what's it gonna cost?

Editor
The professional editor will expect the conversation over money to be a delicate one, and she will recognize any signs of discomfort from the author.

While we might not want to put a price tag on our editing, the truth of the matter is editing is not, should not, and cannot be done for free. If an editor is willing to edit a manuscript for free, the author should be very, very sure that he knows what he is getting at no cost. Professional editors put time and effort into working with authors, and while negotiating a price may be in order, it is hard for an editor to put that price tag on her experience and reliability.

And yet the question remains: How Much? The answer is not so simple but it opens the door to establishing the author/editor relationship. The editor will ask some pertinent questions such as length of the manuscript, fiction, nonfiction, publisher, and deadline. The answers to these and other questions will provide her with information to determine a reasonable cost for the work to be done.

Editorial Expectations

Author

In my experience, the subject of cost rises early in the conversation: "I'm looking for an editor, how much do you charge?" Most authors are not wealthy. They don't have a lot of money to throw around, and yet the smart author should anticipate that a professional edit is not going to be free and will never be wasted money.

When the author begins the search for an editor, he may look at the multitude of websites or book resources or editing groups and will find a variety of answers to the question of cost. One editor might have an opaque listing: $35 an hour, with no explanation as to what that means to the bottom line. Another editor might have a detailed formula that, when data is applied, will tell the author exactly what he can expect to pay. Other editors might fall somewhere in between and list various prices depending upon the service given: proofreading will be less costly than developmental or substantive line editing.

Before this topic of money is left, the author must be comfortable with the answer he has gotten and he should consider all options. If that comfort zone is not reached, he should continue to pursue it. The author should probe any unanswered questions. It is not unreasonable to ask the editor to break down the estimate of the cost.

Contracts

The importance of the contract cannot be understated, as it is a protection for both the author and the editor. As Jon Harrison remarked: "Assuming author and editor have agreed on the scope of the work to be performed and the fee the editor will receive, a last strictly business question remains: whether or not to formalize the relationship with a contract."[5] When the author and editor come to an agreement about working together, each should have a signed copy of the contract.

Editor

As the author and editor interact, any professional, experienced editor will let the author know that there is a contract involved and once each

---

5 *Author and Editor Together: Building the Best Manuscript*, 7

party has agreed to work together, the contract must be signed by both parties before any work begins. If the editor indicates she does not work with a contract and that the proverbial "handshake" is enough, there may be a good reason for that, but the author should be very clear in his understanding if he agrees to no contract.

The contract can be a simple agreement, or it can be a lengthy, detailed legal document, or anything in between. The contract should clearly state the price for the work including any deposit (refundable or nonrefundable), the type of work (proofreading, copyediting, developmental editing, etc.), the deadline for completion (X number of weeks or exact date), any additional charges (editorial reports, printing, cost for revisions, postage, etc.), the manner of work (electronic editing or hard-copy editing), and cancellation and confidentiality clauses.

Author

The author should ask for a blank copy of the contract to review the details before signing, and the editor should expect that request. If the author does not request it, the editor should offer to send it. This action goes a long way toward establishing a sense of trust.

Once it is reviewed, if the author has any questions or concerns, they can be addressed. This will avoid any surprises as the project progresses. Let me repeat . . . the contract protects both the author and the editor. If the editor works without a contract, the author should ask for one as a protection for himself and his intellectual property.

Deadlines

No project should go on without an end date. Knowing the deadline benefits both parties in terms of planning how and when to move the project to the next step.

Editor

Chances are good that an editor will have several projects on her desk at any given time. The editor should anticipate what new work she could handle without jeopardizing contracted work and current clients. Taking on another project, if it jeopardizes work already in the process, is just not a good idea. It's not good for the editor, and it's not good for the author.

As Erin Wilcox states: "When you receive that query about a job that you know isn't the right fit, you'll save everyone valuable time by saying 'No, but thanks for thinking of me.' Possibly the greatest challenge for an independent contractor is saying no to work."[6]

When establishing deadlines, the editor's response will depend on a variety of things including the length of the manuscript, whether it is nonfiction or fiction, the depth of the edit requested by the author, and other projects on his or her desk. The type of edit requested — copyedit, line edit, developmental edit, etc., should be clarified at this time in order for the editor to determine a reasonable deadline for completion as well as cost.

An experienced editor will most likely have a general idea of the time required to complete the project once these questions are answered. A reliable editor will not take on a project just to make money, but will know her limitations in terms of time. If the editor is very interested in the project, she will want to work with the author in order to fit it into her schedule and be able to establish realistic completion dates.

Author

The deadline date will most likely come out during the conversation, but if it is not clear, he should ask or state his expectations for completion. Once the editing begins, the author doesn't just wile away the hours doing nothing. There is marketing to target, a synopsis to write, query letters to prepare, and searching for an agent or publisher, not to mention starting a new book! In order to tie each of these things together, the author will expect a reasonable deadline for the edit to be completed.

A new or inexperienced author will most likely not have any idea of the difference between proofreading, copyediting, or developmental editing. If the author does not understand the different types of edits, the editor must take the time to go over them for clarification, as it may impact the deadline date.

---

6 *Building Successful Freelancer-Client Relationships,* 19

Communication

There are few things that are more important to either a new or an established relationship than a strong communication network.

Editor

It's a good bet that an experienced editor will have more than one project going at any given time. She will have her calendar well organized and will be adept at maneuvering between projects while recognizing deadlines that loom before her. Once the editing has begun, the editor will anticipate working undisturbed and be able to contact the author with any questions that arise. Lack of communication on the part of the editor is a good sign.

Author

Once the editor takes on the job of reading, comprehending, and marking up someone else's work, it is bad form to interrupt that person "just to check up on your progress." Once a deadline has been set, the author should know, regardless of how excited he may be about the editor's expected gushing over his writing, that the editor will be spending a great deal of time looking at every word the author has penned. As mentioned previously, if the editor detects something major in the story that needs attention, she will contact the author and set a time to meet or talk about the issue. If the editor requests a conversation, the author should expect to respond in a timely fashion and be prepared to address any issues that arise.

References

References are important for both the editor and the author. Good references will validate the editor's work skills and deliver a sense of trust to the author.

Editor

There should be an expectation that every author/editor relationship will be a positive one. However, even the most professional of editors will encounter a difficult client—it can't be helped. But professional behavior on the part of the editor with even the most challenging of clients will go a long way toward securing a good reference. A good reference from a previous client will set a comfortable tone for the relationship being established.

Author

The author should ask for references if the editor has not placed them on her website. References will give the author a clear sense of the capabilities of the editor, as well as a chance to get some insight into the pros and cons of working with this particular editor.

In Conclusion . . .

Once the expectations have been raised, discussed, and resolved, the relationship takes on a new life. It is this communication that will move the bond forward into one of trust.

The collaboration between the author and editor should be rewarding and if handled properly, will continue through the years as the author grows in his own experience. The author and editor will learn to regard the other as a friend as well as a successful collaborator. As Betsy Lerner states, ". . . when an editor gives a writer a contract, the effect can be no less intoxicating than the words every lover hopes to hear: *I choose you.*"[7]

Matthew Gartland shares his insight into the job of a great editor with the following checklist created from statements made by Robert Gottlieb in an interview with *The Paris Review*[8]:

1. Be a curator more than a revolutionary.
2. "The editor's relationship to a book should be an invisible one."
3. "The first thing writers want is a quick response." (swift and honest, tempered but tactful)
4. Tell writers not to fear to loosen, open up their writing and be a bit wider.

---

7 *The Forest for the Trees,* 209
8 "The Art of Editing No. 1."

5. "The editorial process will be different for everyone. A good editor responds to the strengths and needs of the writer. Sometimes, if the writer is particularly strong, that's just offering encouragement."
6. Writers are like actors, they need "directors" (an editor) to tell them where they're strong and where they're weak to get the best out of them.
7. **Editing is largely a profession of perspective.** "What you really want in an editor is someone who's still on the dock, who can say, 'Hi, I'm looking at your ship, and it's missing a bow, the front mast is crooked, and it looks to me as if your propellers are going to have to be fixed.'"
8. **"Your job as an editor is to figure out what the book needs, but the writer has to provide it."**
9. "No editor should work with a book he doesn't like, because his job as an editor is to make something better of what it is."
10. As an editor, "your job with [an overly passionate and stubborn] writer is to be able to say, 'You may have done an equally brilliant job on all of these things, but this has more weight than that, and you have to give some of that up.'"
11. "It is best NOT to layer another sensibility or another vocabulary on top of what's already written," but instead "get inside the text and instinctively understand the terms and the vocabulary of the writer, and make changes in those terms and that vocabulary."
12. ". . . the most strained moments in books are the very beginning and the very end—the getting in and the getting out."
13. The ending is especially awkward. ". . . sometimes the most useful thing you can tell a writer is, 'Here's where the book ends.'"
14. **Writers need to be told when their books are bad.**[9]

The relationship is a success . . . all because expectations were raised, discussed, and resolved.

---

9 "The Robert Gottlieb Guide to Editing, My Personal Notes"

Bibliography

Gartland, Matthew. "The Robert Gottlieb Guide to Editing, My Personal Notes." Winning Edits LLC (2012). http://winningedits.com.

Gottlieb, Robert. "The Art of Editing No. 1." Interview by Larissa MacFarquhar. *The Paris Review*, Fall, 1994.

Harrison, Jon. *Authors and Editors Together: Building the Best Manuscript.* New York: Editorial Freelancers Association, 2016.

Lerner, Betsy. *The Forest for the Trees.* New York: *River Head Books*, 2000.

Wilcox, Erin. *Building Successful Freelancer-Client Relationships.* New York: Editorial Freelancers Association, 2016.

About the Author

Judith (Judy) Reveal was born in Chicago in 1945. Libraries and reading and writing have always been her passion. She spent 40 years wandering the corridors of Corporate America where business writing honed her skills including editing, proofing, and just plain writing. She has taught creative writing and currently freelances as a manuscript editor, a book reviewer (nyjournalofbooks.com) and a book indexer. Her book, *The Four Elements of Fiction: Character, Setting, Situation, and Theme* is a guide for newer writers who need a place to start. She is active in a variety of organizations including Eastern Shore Writers' Association, Bay To Ocean Writers' Conference, Howard County Writers Conference, and Vine and Vessels Writers Conference.

www.ingramcontent.com/pod-product-compliance
Lightning Source LLC
Chambersburg PA
CBHW070120110526
44587CB00016BA/2742